BREATHLESS

The Unspoken Truth

KAMI KOTOBI

Copyright © 2012 Kami Kotobi

All rights reserved.

ISBN: **0615733883**
ISBN-13: **978-0615733883 (Kami's Corner)**

DEDICATION

In loving memory of my beloved father

CONTENTS

PROLOGUE 1

LET THE DREAMER DREAM 4

BREATHLESS 5

DREAM 7

A RECOLLECTION 8

DO YOU KNOW WHO I AM? 10

NOTHING TO DECLARE 11

KISS 12

TEARS NEVER SHED 13

BITTERSWEET 14

A LIFE LIVED 15

THE GLASS CASTLE 16

ZIN 17

SWALLOW'S FLIGHT 18

PEDDLER CHILD 20

CANARY 22

WOMAN 23

VINTAGE WINE 25

HAVE YOU EVER? 26

UNTIL THE LAST MOMENT 28

FROM ME TO MY HEART 30

STORY UNTOLD 32

DANCE OF DESIRE 33

I FEEL YOU 34

THE SHADOW OF YOUR SMILE	35
AS I DREAM	37
AWOVAL	38
CONFESSION	39
A WISH	40
I, THE MIRROR, OR MY OWN REFLECTION?	41
TRAPPED	43
WHERE WERE YOU?	44
LIFE IN YOUR YEARS	46
DAYDREAM	47
I HAVE NOT FORGOTTEN	48
HOW DO I FEEL?	50
COLD SHOULDER	52
FACES	54
SELF WITHIN	56
WRITER'S BLOCK	58
A LOOK WITHIN	59
DARE TO LIVE	61
SOLITUDE	63
LOSE YOURSELF	65
NOW	66
FORGOTTEN!	67

ACKNOWLEDGMENTS

I would like to thank and acknowledge the following individuals for their contributions to this book:

Dina Dinari – Book Cover Design
www.dinaridesign.com
dina@dinaridesign.com

Saeed Zargham – Front cover photo
Alfa Image Photography
www.alfaimagephotography.com
alfaimagephotography@yahoo.com

Marmar Esmaeili Nia – Back cover photo

Ramin Ghazi - Subtitle

PROLOGUE

I thought of heaven and hell a fool's dream…
an old wives' tale…
My heaven and hell were here on earth, now I see…
I see…

From the point in time in which a fertilized egg splits into two for the very first time, to the very last seconds in which we exhale our last breath, our lives are shaped, touched, felt, and lived through a series of defining moments:

The exhilarating moment when we, as children, realized that we were riding the bicycle, for but a split second, unassisted and without the training wheels...

The moment of our first kiss and how strange yet delicious and warm it felt sending millions of tingling shocks of electricity through every cell of our bodies...

The first time we made love, not just with our physical bodies, but with our SOULS...

The moment in which a newborn's tiny little hand wraps around a single finger of her exhausted mother and makes it all worthwhile...

The moment when a parent hears "dada" or "mama" for the first time...

The moment when we know, with every shred of our being that we are in love...

Of course life is not that kind and generous to bestow upon us only moments of utter and sheer happiness. We feel pain, we feel the unbearable and the deafening silence of loneliness, we feel sorrow, we cry, we become ill, we experience defeats, disappointments and loss.

And so we should!

For it is the existence and the experience of sorrow, pain, loneliness, defeat, disappointment, and loss that give us the frame of reference, the perspective and the contrast needed to truly appreciate and treasure, laughter, happiness, triumph, beauty in the most minute of things, and love.

We, live our lives, each in our own special and unique way, to covet, to seek, to find, to create, to collect, and even sometimes to steal as many beautiful and meaningful moments as we can. And, we wear these treasured moments like beautiful and priceless charms on the bracelets of our lives!

At the end, it matters not how long we have lived. What matters is the number of charms hanging off of our bracelets of life!!!!!

BREATHLESS

LET THE DREAMER DREAM

Take me far
Far from these judging eyes;
and let me be.
No longer a sinner among sinners;
set me free.

A supplication,
wrapped neatly in a silent scream
echoes from the chasm of wakefulness;
"Let the dreamer dream"...

BREATHLESS

Quiet my mind, I cannot,
for I am restless;
haunted still, by my last image of you,
I am feeble, I am helpless.

I dreamed of you in my arms,
forever sheltered;
a dream that shattered so soon,
leaving me broken, baffled and bewildered.

A gift of life anew,
was our embrace;
but the bitter truth,
soon, I came to face.

Sweet tomorrow,
a dream fulfilled, I used to say;
the cruel tomorrow came,
and it took you away!

A thousand ways to kill a man,
it is no lie;
for there are so many ways
for me to die.

I was a fool,
little did I know;
soon, my end would come,
a death agonizing, and ever so slow.

Quiet my mind, I cannot,
for I am restless;
our love, my last breath of hope,
stolen from me mercilessly,
leaving me gasping and breathless…

DREAM

To speak in dreams…
To summon her to your subconscious realm
To shed the mask, and to be seen…
Fantasies that overwhelm

How divine to be undying and ceaseless
For as long as in her dreams I dwell!

A RECOLLECTION

Heart races,
mind is swallowed in a spiral of delight,
as she
calls her lover's name.

Passion boils to an upsurge
when the desire is confessed.

Fingertips engaged in a seductive dance...
Lips savoring...
Breath, gasping…
A thousand delicious tingles,
one more intense than its precursor.

Bodies merging,
skin on skin.
Chests heaving,
forms wrapped,
souls emerging!

Delightful sounds
confessing innate pleasure.
Intensity beyond description,
testament to the depth of desire.

Lovers embracing fervently
in fear of separation!
A moment savored,

the next anticipated...

Moment after moment,
togetherness reaches a new height.
Bodies dance,
souls soar ...
A storm brews within,
they can hear it roar.

The brush kisses the canvas with a gentle touch
She, the vessel...
Colors emerging,
brilliant and bright.

Hands clench in anticipation,
bodies collapse,
soul runs through soul,
as two
become one!

The past, erased;
meaningless, is what to come.
Here and now,
they are,
together
in a moment
that lasts a lifetime!

DO YOU KNOW WHO I AM?

When your eyes ferret me out through the howling throng
What do you see?
Whom do you see?
Do you know who I am?

When I return your gaze with a smile
What do you see?
Whom do you see?
Do you know who I am?

You read my written words
You trace my brush stokes on the finished canvas
My footprints on the encrusted road
Yet you haven't walked my path
Do you know who I am?

What you see, just a glimpse
What you witness, a fleeting moment
Only a two-bit puzzle can be solved
when you have but two bits
Do you know who I am?

Answer me not in haste
Abandon all conventions engrained
Shed the fitting cloak of judgment
And only then, speak your heart
Do you know who I am?

NOTHING TO DECLARE

Moment of truth
Emotions run high
Self-conscious perhaps
A single sigh, my tearless cry

In this passage, I walk alone
Knowing now what I should have known
All along and through it all,
there is no climb without a fall

Engaged in a journey I did not plan,
the passing scenery, I probingly scan
Parallel tracks that never end...
This wound too, time will mend

Shoulders saddled,
one too often frets
Burdens I carry,
coffers of secrets

Somewhere between distant and looming
is yet another judgment at hand
Time to be bold,
for tall I must stand

No room for regrets,
no time for despair;
this gate too, I shall pass
Nothing to declare…
Nothing to declare…

KISS

Her scent, I devoured and consumed with lust;
as the touch of her hand ran through me with an
implausible thrust.

To my innermost instincts, I surrendered and caved;
for the taste of her mouth, all night, I had craved.

In her warm eyes, I saw my own reflection;
as I held her close with such fervor and conviction.

I my arms at last, every kiss, I prolonged and
belabored
I tasted her mouth, and every kiss, I relished and
Savored

Sweet melody I heard as she called my name
The wild beast in me, in her embrace, now tame!

TEARS NEVER SHED

Letters written
Never read
Tears cried
Never shed

Too far apart to embrace
Bitter truth, they shall face

Their love, never meant to be
She knew it not, and nor did he

Letters written, each a plea
Wishing his sorrow she would see

He beseeched and he implored
While every letter, she ignored

In her silence, years passed and perished
His fading recollection, all that he cherished

Letters written
Never read
Tears cried
Never shed!

BITTERSWEET

The sad song plays, endlessly, on repeat
Like belligerent vine, the lyrics wrap around my head
Each word a thorn, on this crown of defeat

Unhurriedly, the wall of silence is crumbling inside
Echoes I hear, in every darkened corner of my mind
Voices I hear, filled with nothing but lie and deceit

Drowning in sorrow, searching thought the past
I hold back the tears; for no man cries
Burdened with self-reproach, my desperate heart, I so poorly treat

Lost in this song of ghosts past
I am nothing; yet am all that there is!
Solitude, ever constant, ever present, bittersweet…

A LIFE LIVED

A life lived,
many years cherished,
many wasted.

The fruit of youth,
those delightful years,
savored and tasted.

Laughter and tears,
defeats and triumphs,
through them all,
I've been tried and tested.

My heart,
inexorable and relentless,
yet broken many times over,
when it was the least expected!

My face,
withered and scared;
and the burden of it all,
deep within these wrinkles,
it has nested.

Future fuddled and obscure
I know not what may come;

standing tall, I will remain,
for I am far too invested!

THE GLASS CASTLE

From every angle the brilliant light reflects;
mesmerized by the glamor, the hidden truth, the eye neglects.

Built high above to reach the skies;
this glass castle, is but a façade, a disguise.

Intruding light, broken into prisms by crystal walls
Punishingly cold, with empty rooms and empty halls

Locked inside by her own will,
is the woman sitting by the windowsill.

Chosen to be its crowned queen;
she was but a girl, her years, only seventeen.

Decades have passed, the wine has aged
She wanders the halls, her heart is caged

Still a dreamer, concealing her scars;
she stares above, and counts the stars!

Filled with regret, fright and rage;
no longer willing to play center stage.

Her mind races, her heart beating fast;
wishing for her to break this golden cast.

She longs to be free, free at last
Soring the skies blue and vast…

ZIN

I, an intoxicated believer,
recall that seductive bottle of zin.
Rich in color, taste of spice;
sleeping underneath it all, hints of hedonistic sin!

A dark liquid portrait of a poet;
a potent combination, hard edges and soft touch.
Sending me into a trance;
beyond a dream, I can't recall much.

It's deep complexity, tingles the senses
Utter bliss
Sweet, warm, and rousing,
reminiscent of my very first kiss.

SWALLOW'S FLIGHT

Perching on a red roof tile, sat the bird swallow;
pondering her faith, deciding,
whether the flock or her defiant heart to follow.

In that hour of wind and light,
the brave swallow took her flight.

She soared high in the vast sky
Unwavering and steadfast
Abandoning consensus,
and convention of generations past.

Aiming for the distant land
Far in the west
Dreaming only of warmth,
and of her new clay nest!

Days and nights, she spent in flight;
no one knows of her pain and plight.

Dashing in the skies with rapid wing,
only to a dream, her heart would cling.

Beneath the rain bearing clouds,
the light of moon, her path guides.

Of her fate, no one knows;
but my eagerness,

it still grows.

She will arrive one day soon;
I'll see her in the skies beneath the moon.

Arriving home, tired and weary;
now in the past, a life dreary.

On my roof the brave little swallow will land;
the cherished moment, her ultimate aim, finally at hand.

Once again,
perching on a red roof tile,
The brave swallow will make me smile…

PEDDLER CHILD

Far too close,
to the street peddler,
a speeding car passes by.

In an instant startled;
in a fleeting second stunned.

The wild flower bouquet,
meets the punishing pavement,
as his weary hand loses its grip.

Shaking,
abashed and ashamed,
fretted and teary eyed;
scattered flowers,
he endeavors to salvage,
in haste.

What we see, you and I,
dispersed,
in red and yellow,
is far from what his eyes see!

Worthless wildflowers,
to you and I;
livelihood, pride,
a proud mother's smile,
to this peddler child.

BREATHLESS

Petals crushed,
smeared and smashed,
his descending tears kiss;
tears of shame,
a child remiss!

...

Fragile and frail,
is life to us all.
Hangs by a reedy thread,
our fate after all!

CANARY

Behold, you beholder, behold!
The story of the caged "canary" is but once told.

What beauty do your eyes see
when you gaze through the bars?

What music do you hear
when the interned canary cries?

Canary, canary, caged for all to see
Canary, canary, how you long to be free

...

Her story, one and of the same kind;
Beautiful on the outside,
though forever trapped,
behind the bars of her own mind!

WOMAN

Woman
Your voice,
soothing music of angels,
echoes in the depths of my soul.

Woman
Your skin,
a meadow in the garden of Eden…

Woman
I, filled with desire,
and you,
a beacon,
calling me home.

Woman
Your touch,
soft,
warm,
and yet electrifying;
pushing me to the edge of insanity!

Woman
I trace your every curve;
they captivate
and seduce my senses.

Woman
Your scent
I inhale,
"a warm summer breeze"!!!

VINTAGE WINE

With a lover's touch, I hold the slender bottle in my grip
The silky ale, teasing my senses, seducing me, sip after sip

The sweet vintage wine flows through every vein
Washing away the scum of this nagging pain

Though the effect, impermanent, short lived and brief
I relish every second, free of the weight of this grief

Impermanence and frailty, give way to immortality
As one after another, dissipate these layers of reality

Drunken and intoxicated, adrift, I float away
Amid the conscious and the subconscious I sway

The light shines through, waning and decay no more
Weightless and buoyant, a feather, briskly I soar

With a lover's touch, I hold the slender bottle in my grip
I, a traveler, the sweet wine, my only companion on this trip!

HAVE YOU EVER?

Have you ever?
Have you ever felt so alone,
that your own reflection in the mirror was company?

Have you ever?
Have you ever felt so much anger, rage and fury,
that your fingertips felt as though they were going to explode?

Have you ever?
Have you ever been so suffocated in silence,
that your own skin felt like a shackled restraint?

Have you ever?
Have you ever entombed so much disappointment,
that the decaying stench of it made you bilious?

Have you ever?
Have you ever?
…

The hopeful and buoyant reflection in the mirror calls:

Tomorrow, is yet a new day…
Once more,
you will wash away the corrosion of day past.
Once more,
you will go to your closet of masks,

and put on a new façade for the day anew!

Tomorrow, is yet a new day…
Yet, a new stage…
To play the fictitious "brave"!

Mystified and baffled,
at my reflection I gaze;
and my own voice echoes once more

Tomorrow, is yet a new day…
A new day to scream in silence!

UNTIL THE LAST MOMENT

Fleeting and ever evanescent,
Frailty and fragility lie beneath your hardened shell;
more of you, I cannot steal or bargain,
for no one will ever sell!

Around each familiar corner and beneath the shadows of uncertainty,
self assured, I travel fast;
yet, fearful of the inevitable eventuality!

No beacon to guide me home and no compass to show the way
I walk this maze, amazed at its enormity, adrift and astray

My aim, ever-changing or set in stone
The end of this tale, no one has ever known

Steadfast and unwavering, I steer this ship this way and that;
in this enigmatic and inscrutable game, who is the mouse, and who is the cat?

Answers I seek in every step of the way
Choices infinite, the right path, who is to say?

Disdain or reverence?
Admiration or contempt?

Utterly in awe and filled with wonderment;
I, a pendulum,
vacillating between clarity and bewilderment.

Yet, unyielding and obstinate,
I recommence and persist.
Until the last moment,
surrender or defeat, I will resist…

FROM ME TO MY HEART

From me to my heart…

Tonight, and in this moment of solitude,
free of wantedness,
sheltered from the falling rain of desire,
naked and bare, without the armor of pride,
and unshackled from lust,
I speak to you humbled, for confess to you, I must.

In our run, and thus far in our pursuits,
we have been relentless;
selfish, perhaps at times,
but our nature, still selfless.

We have had our share
of both, fair and unfair

We have been beaten, and we have seen defeat
We have seen trickery, and we have seen deceit
We have been deserted and scorned
Through it all, together, you and I have mourned

My face has aged, and my hair ashen
No choice, for we all have to take our ration

Broken and blemished, yet unyielding and resolute
You have walked by my side in this pursuit

Your fractures,
scars of my defeats,
marks of my blunders and missteps;
wear them with honor as I do this graying hair.

Your forgiveness I seek my beloved heart
You, my faithful companion
We will never be apart...!

STORY UNTOLD

Ask me
Who are you?
And I shall tell you who I aspire to be

Ask me where I have come from
And I shall tell you what has brought me here

Ask me why I am here
And I shall tell you where I have been

Ask me how I feel
And I shall tell you about a scream caged in silence

Ask me what I believe in
And I shall tell you how I lost all faith!

Ask me
Ask me my name
And I shall tell you a story untold…

DANCE OF DESIRE

When fingertips are filled with curiosity
When pupils dilate ravenously for maximum exposure
When the skin itches for a single touch
When lips thirst for a single kiss
When the slightest glimpse and the most subtle of curves become potent aphrodisiacs
When hearts beat restlessly in anticipation of togetherness
Time and space lose all meaning
Senses heighten and feral imagination reigns
Intoxicating delight runs through the veins of two bodies
Yearning to join together in a blissful dance of desire!

I FEEL YOU

In every drop of rain,
in every wave of the ocean,
and in every gentle breeze,
I feel you…

Under the blanket of the morning fog,
in the purple clouds of each sunset,
and in every flicker of light in the night sky,
I feel you…

In the beat of my own heart,
in the silence of my solitude,
I feel you…

At the height of ecstasy or the depth of anguish,
I feel vibrant and effervescent;
simply because,
I feel you…

No greater treasure,
than to have you flow in my veins;
no higher privilege,
than to share every breath…

I feel YOU!

THE SHADOW OF YOUR SMILE

Stranded in this asylum
all that keeps me sane
the shadow of your smile…

My only companion
in the abyss of lonely nights
the shadow of your smile…

The only cure
that mends this broken heart
the shadow of your smile…

Painting vivid colors
over my darkened dreams
the shadow of your smile…

When memory lapses and all is but a blur,
I remember still
the shadow of your smile…

When lost in the vastness of my plight,
my only beacon,
the shadow of your smile…

In the coldness of my solitude,
warming my heart with tingling sparkles of love
the shadow of your smile…

When a kiss is but a dream and when your hand is out of reach;
I close my eyes, and summon to me
the shadow of your smile…

No misfortune of any significance or substance;
my life, opulent and sumptuous
for as I long as I can recall
the shadow of your smile!

AS I DREAM

Slowly roused from a solemn slumber
No longer dreaming,
but yet, still lost in a dream

Heedless of time, neglectful of my surroundings
I strain to hold onto the images that rush through my mind's eye
Sweet remnants of a reverie
Passing by just as fast as they vanish from my conscious memory for ever

Unreservedly, I float in endless time and space
Unleashed from the perils of the conscious mind

At the core, I am one with the essence…
Nay, I AM the essence!

Time, futile and meaningless
I am untainted and unalloyed

Drowned and saturated with utter love
I am immersed in a dance
with YOU!

AWOVAL

Steering clear from inevitable judgment, for years have been I…
Ever so pleasing, to known and unknown, seeker of approval have been I…

Reclusive at heart and at the core, time after time, the center stage have taken I…
Wearing mask after mask and acting the part, building a wall have been I….

No longer, no further, and never more
This ship has sailed its voyage; now at the shore

I have arrived, liberated and free
No masks remaining, nothing but ME!

To you spectators of life, Judge me as you wish
I am free of you; it is only truth that I now cherish

Make believe happiness no more; the wall will go no further
My own sense of self, I no longer will murder!

CONFESSION

It's 2:30 in the morning, no one in sight;
sitting in a corner, I'm filled with fright.

My heart is heavy, confess I must;
to you, and to myself, I have to be just.

Far too eager, in your eyes, I appear aloof, distant and cold;
in truth, it took all that I could muster to be so bold!

Inside, I am as broken as you;
not knowing what to think, say, or do.

Life goes on, as usual, and with the same speed;
keeping pace, now, is much harder indeed.

For you, what I had to do, I did…
Vanity, egotism and selfishness, I forbid

I hope someday, clearly, you will see
How it broke my heart to set you free!

A WISH

I am befuddled and conflicted
I am blameless, yet convicted!

Like a leaf floating on a river
My life thus far, has wandered and drifted

The weight and burden of life
I wish it lifted

Garbled memories and thoughts
I wish them sifted

Lucidity and clarity I seek
Only if I were that gifted!

I, THE MIRROR, OR MY OWN REFLECTION?

I, a stranger, even to my own self it seems;
as I sit in solitude and stare at my own reflection.

Details blur and blur even more, illegible and unfamiliar
How did I ever come to deserve this affliction?

I have traveled this road, so long and so far
An accomplished traveler to many, yet unacquainted with my own destination

Who am I, and what purpose do I serve?
What were the significance and the consequence of my conception?

A son, a brother, a friend, or a lover?
The creator or the creation?
Playing the part in the theater of life…
Engrossed and obsessed with utter perfection

Mind, body and soul, intermingled into an indecipherable illusion
This trinity, my golden cage;
how can I break free from this triangulation?

Agonizing search for the truth of it all, these days, my only companion

Determined, and yet uncertain of the merit of my own dissertation

When the observer is observed, and the perceiver perceived;
which is existent, genuine and real?
I, the mirror, or my won reflection?!

TRAPPED

Present time halted, tomorrow concealed
Can't see the future, for the past

Memories, haunting me still
How long will the dreadful nightmare last?

Broken, into infinite pieces, little by little
Whole on the outside, and yet, lost in this cosmic vast…

Trusting?
No longer and never more
My faith in purity and propriety, I'm losing fast!

Fatigued and weary of self reflection,
yet in this mirror I still gaze
Trapped inside myself, wishing desperately to break this cast!

WHERE WERE YOU?

Where were you
when I cried out your name,
and heard not even my own echo?

Where were you
when I walked in haste and bewildered among the crowds;
every face bearing your likeness, and yet
you were no where to be found?

Where were you
when a kind word uttered through your sweet lips
was the only remedy to my ill faded affliction?

Where were you
when lost in thought and lost in time,
I watched days slip into nights and nights into days;
as I stared through the window of my memories?

Burned and broken, void of all pride,
a fetus, crouched in a corner of an empty room;
I took refuge in the womb of your silence…

Where were you?
Where were you?
Where were you?

My incubation, pain and sorrow;

my gestation, mourning and regret.
A seedling of change,
I was reborn,
an orphan!

LIFE IN YOUR YEARS

Seven thousand, or seven miles
Paved with tears and paved with smiles

Soaring heights, arcane depths
The road of life, beneath my steps

This wondrous road, we travel fast
Too little time, the scenery vast

From, and to others, we give and take
This conventional pattern, we hardly break

Along this road, we slave and save
To leave it all for a darkened grave!

All in all, and in the end,
know this secret my cherished friend

What counts in your life, is not the years
It is rather, the LIFE in your years!

DAYDREAM

It's one of those days when you just want to walk in the sun
And I am lost in a daydream…

I am lost in her eyes
I am lost in her smile
I walk in a daze
I walk for a while

The world passes by as fast as ever;
and I can see it in the corners of my eyes.
It may pass me by, and I don't care
Opening my eyes, I can't and I don't dare
She is by my side in this sweet dream;
and that's all that matters now.

It's one of those days when you just want to walk in the sun
And I am lost in a daydream…

Floating free, on this warm river of love
I will dream this dream into the night!

I HAVE NOT FORGOTTEN

Together, and yet so far apart you and I
In love still, but we struggle you and I
Hearts filled with love and yet broken
The silence deafening, so much left unspoken

Building walls against it all to shelter
Our deeds pragmatic, fearful not to falter
Denying the heart, just to survive
Against a love that cries to thrive

Life goes on empty and cold
Fearful as ever, and yet so bold
Our wings broken, incapable of flight
With memories we live each day and night

Through it all, wrong or right
A flame burns still, ever so bright!
A confession, left unspoken…
Despite of it all, I have not forgotten!

How I trembled when you were near
How my aim was so clear
How your hand felt in mine
How a kiss was so divine
How it felt when we embraced
How my claim on you I traced
How complete you made me feel
How those dreams we made so real…

Of us, who knows what will become
No one can foretell, the future to come
Although, wrong or right, I cannot distinguish
Your love, I know, I won't relinquish

Forever dissolved within my blood
I surrender to this overwhelming flood
As long as blood flows in these veins
Yours, my heart forever remains!

Our future austere, or at least uncertain
Despite of it all, my beloved, I have not forgotten!

HOW DO I FEEL?

With all that has been said and done…
With all that has come and gone…

Doubtful and unsure, teary-eyed, yet reluctant
You say you don't know how I feel!

Tongue-tied and at a loss for words, I may be at times,
but you know how I feel…

My thoughts, consumed by you
And you know how I feel…

I long for you like no other
And you know how I feel…

My love for you grows stronger still
And you know how I feel…

With you complete, ever so content
And you know how I feel…

Without you, I'm lost
And you know how I feel…

Safe and complete, when you are near
And you know how I feel…

BREATHLESS

Every minute apart, an eternity
And you know how I feel…

Every kiss, every touch, a treasure
And you know how I feel…

I found heaven in your embrace
And you know how I feel…

Filled with life or buried under,
I am forever yours
And you know how I feel...

You are my destination, you are my home!
And you know how I feel…

You, my opiate; and I, an eternal addict
You know how I feel…

Flows in my veins, this love for you
Grows stronger with every beat of my heart
You have given me life anew, and I am ALIVE!
And that is how I feel!

COLD SHOULDER

I fell hard for you, no choice of my own
In this web, two innocent hearts were thrown
With every passing moment, with every touch
My love and fervor for you have grown

I gave you my heart, I gave you my soul
I did so gladly, and I will do it all over again
I've lost my grip, I've lost all control
In love with you eternally, I will remain

Loving me is not easy, I know
Your saddened and tired face, testament to its toll
Too little or too much, I've given you all I have to give
It's not enough, for you deserve so much more…

Fire within burns hot while the outer shell grows colder
Don't give up; don't give me your cold shoulder!

…

You breathe life into me, you nourish my soul
Without your love, nothing's left but heartache and pain
You abandoned out there, and I here on my own
In the ashes of this separation, our memories are all that remain!

Despite of it all, so much strength our love has shown
Desperately seeking ways, struggling our passion to regain
Reason and desire in an eternal brawl
Out of this struggle, we cannot crawl

Loving me is not easy, I know
Your saddened and tired face, testament to its toll
Too little or too much, I've given you all I have to give
It's not enough, for you deserve so much more...

Fire within burns hot while the outer shell grows colder
Don't give up, don't give me your cold shoulder!

FACES

Faces I wear, far too many
Their tally and disposition not known by any

These gaudy masks, perhaps, a measure of protection
Safeguards against judgments, inferences and rejection

Free, we may seem to be; but our hands are often tied
Drowned in diverge realities, forgetful of when we were truthful and when we lied

In the mirror, at my own self I gaze
In search of a way, out of this maze

An image, mystified, bewildered and confound
I find myself, drained, burdened and bound

Marks and scars, I see in this reflection
Footsteps of time, a common ill-fated affliction

Self discovery, indeed a harsh trek
Summing your life into an insignificant speck!

Vulnerable, exposed, naked and bare
Concealment and perjury, you no longer dare

Not easy to hide all these feelings inside
Much consequence, too many rules to abide

True meaning I seek through it all
Nothing else matters, after all…

SELF WITHIN

The voice within, calls…
His voice, echoing in the empty halls

There is no hell or heaven
Your sins, they all, will be forgiven

Rules, break free from their binding chain
Selfishly, your uninhibited freedom regain

Far too short, is this life, indeed
Claim it with passion, lust and greed

In the dark, I sit down and think
Bottle in hand, I drown and drink…

Starring into the distance, answers I seek
Scenery before me, desolate and bleak

What has come of my goodness?, I ask
How long will I bear this tainted mask?

Engaged in an eternal dual with the self within…
Tempted, eager, yet fearful of this sin

Not the only one, in this struggle engaged

Am I the sanest, or troubled and deranged?

What future may bring, I cannot foretell
Here and now, are my heaven and hell!

WRITER'S BLOCK

Lately, I find myself silent and tongue-tied
Unable to express any thoughts, no matter how hard I've tried
From one thought to the next, my mind races still…
No longer can I let the words flow at will

This too, will pass I'm sure
But this unwelcomed guest I cannot ignore

Screams I hear from the depths of my mind
Distracted, battered and stifled, by the daily grind

So many thoughts left unsaid and so much left to confess
So many doubts and so many fears left to express

Eyes fixed on the virgin paper, pen in hand
Motionless and wilted, I daydream of a distant land

Thousand images rush passed in a constant progression
I, a paralyzed spectator, unable to break this regression!

Have I already said what had to be said?
Have I woven the web to the end of my thread?

Silently I in this corner I sit, listening to my heart weep and cry
My muse, without you the tongue is tied and the ink is dry…

A LOOK WITHIN

There are thoughts I do not dare
with my closest kin, even share

Some are dark, and some are bright
Filled with hope, filled with fright

Weary that I might be judged
Too vain and too proud to be ascertained!

Others are but a mirror for you to see
who and what, you have become to be

Too ugly at times, maybe
my reflection, even too callous for me!

Too self absorbed as the next, truth to be told
No more or less giving, but honest, brutal and bold

Too proud and egotistical to follow
The religious poison, I refuse to swallow!

In heaven or in hell will I reside?
Whose rules will I abide?

Whose is the hand that holds the string?
Fate of us all, who will bring?

Who should I be, which path should I take?
Will I sell out, my soul forsake?

My beliefs, for ages instilled
In my brain, eternally ingrained

How will we ever know?
What will we have for ourselves to show?

What is my purpose, what legacy will I leave behind?
Will the judgment be fair, evenhanded and kind?

Unanswered questions, far too many
Source of truth, I know not of any

Believe in one, If I must
only myself, I can trust!

Instinct, wisdom and compassion
my guiding lights through this progression

Adaptive, strong, and filled with love
I aspire to be, all above!

DARE TO LIVE

I often wonder
what of me will remain?

I often wonder
will it be a loss or a gain?

Is there a purpose to living this life?
Or, will it all perish in vain?

Futile exercise it seems
but I cannot refrain

Some believe in heaven and hell
and this belief, they faithfully maintain

Blind faith, a chronic excuse
Unwilling to question, unable to explain!

Following the path of least resistance
Devoted, committed, yet insane!

Ironic, this game of life
The answers hidden, they forever remain

I know not the answer, nor mastery I claim
A cynical seeker, filled with inquisitive thoughts I cannot contain

I know what I know, and I know what I don't…
Slave of contentment, I haven't been, and I won't!

Life is too short, a cliché, I know
My passion for life, forever will grow

The beauty, is the mystery of the unknown
An intricate puzzle, so many pieces not shown!

With each passing moment, the hunger mounts
It is not the destination, but the journey that counts

Dare to live, to the very last
Learn from your sacred past

Embrace what comes, break the rigid cast
Swim in the ocean of life, for it is vast

Dare to live, to the very last
For in a blink of any eye,
your "future" is your "past"!

Every minute, every second, a gift
Make them last, make them last…

SOLITUDE

The room is dark
void of light

Senses heightened
but no sight

My eyes closed, my face a frown
Random thoughts, left and right…

Glass of ale, empty almost
Helping to lessen my fright

Afraid of what has been
and what might

The war is not yet over
So many battles left to fight!

The taste is bitter
Jaws clench tight

As the dark liquid burns
Thoughts sore to a new height

The mind's eye opens
in search of light!
Your image comes to mind
Pure sense of delight!

A new sense of consciousness I gain
as the warm ale passes through each vein

As surroundings become more blur
ever so self aware I remain

As I slowly shed the fear
a peaceful calm I gain

The present dissolves more with every sip
Reality vanishes as I lose my grip!

Intoxicated by the thoughts of you, and not the ale
These thoughts, like fresh air, I inhale

The peace that overcomes me is beyond compare
No longer do I feel the sadness, fear, or despair

In flesh, in my thoughts, or in my dreams
you are the only answer it seems!

The past, present, or the future matter none
as I forsake all others but one!

LOSE YOURSELF

The darkness falls, the silent moon aglow;
dark shadows of doubt, in every corner they grow.
Exposed, cold, naked and bare
Sinking deep in the quicksand of despair

Unendingly struggling, pushed this way and that
A helpless pawn, recurrently pulled to and fro
I am no stranger to your pain;
for your aching soul,
like my very own, I know.

I see the tears that you so restrain;
look into my eyes, and
let your tears flow!

I have feared what you dread the most;
take my hand in yours, and
let your fears go.

Stand with me upon this edge of insanity
The dark valley below, beckoning with such vanity

Through your very core, let my words flow:
"Lose yourself, be set free, and let yourself go!"

NOW

No matter how potent and inebriating,
a broken chalice holds no ale…

Here and now, my only dominion;
when the past is to be forgotten, and tomorrow forlorn…

Life, an impermanent temple indeed;
and I, the pilgrim, the deity, and the priest!!!

FORGOTTEN!

I am nothing but a feeble flame;
not a pawn
nor a hand in this cruel of a game.

I am nothing but a brilliant flash of light;
short lived,
dashing across the skies of a star studded night.

I am but a drop in this ocean vast;
seen for but a fleeting moment,
and forgotten just as fast!

…

www.ingramcontent.com/pod-product-compliance
Lightning Source LLC
Chambersburg PA
CBHW031210090426
42736CB00009B/865